G000095265

COCKTAILS

COCKTAILS

DAVID BIGGS

PHOTOGRAPHY BY
ANTHONY JOHNSON

CRESCENT BOOKS
NEW YORK • AVENEL

This 1995 edition published by Crescent Books,
distributed by Random House Value Publishing, Inc.,
40 Engelhard Avenue, Avenel, New Jersey 07001.

Random House
New York • Toronto • London • Sydney • Auckland

Originally published in the UK in 1994 by
New Holland (Publishers) Ltd

A CIP calalog for this book is available from the
Library of Congress

ISBN 0-517-14244-9

Editors: Linda de Villiers and Coral Walker
Design concept: Janice Evans
In-house designer: Peter Bosman
Assistant designers: Petal Palmer and Lellyn Creamer
Photographer: Anthony Johnson
Stylist: Vo Pollard

Typesetting by Suzanne Fortescue, Struik DTP
Reproduction by Hirt and Carter
Printed and bound in Singapore by Tien Wah Press (Pte) Ltd

❖ ❖ ❖ ❖ ❖ ❖ ❖ ❖ ❖ ❖

CONTENTS

INTRODUCTION

Legend has it that the cocktail was invented by Betsy Flanagan, an Irish inn-keeper in America. She created exciting mixtures of drinks which she served from bottles gaily decorated with the tail feathers of roosters.

A French customer is said to have raised his glass to toast the wonderful drink he was enjoying, and declared: *"Vive le cocktail!"* giving the mixed drink its name.

The name could also have been derived from "cock-ale," which was a mixture of alcoholic drinks fed to fighting cocks to give them courage.

Whatever their origin, cocktails came into their own during the American Prohibition years of the 1920s and 30s. Illicit "moonshine" stills often produced liquor of very dubious quality, and these concoctions sometimes needed all the help they could get, to make them palatable. This led, naturally, to a wide range of interesting mixtures, some of which (like the Martini and the Manhattan) earned immortality as classic cocktails.

When Prohibition was repealed in 1933, the standard of liquor improved enormously, but cocktails had come to stay as an essential part of sophisticated life.

Today there are literally thousands of different cocktails, and each of them has its local variations. Whatever the experts may claim, there is no right or wrong way of making a particular cocktail. Cocktail enthusiasts will urge their friends to go to this or that bar, "where Ernie mixes the greatest dry Martini in the world." Obviously Ernie's recipe is likely to be slightly different from anybody else's. And this is the magic of the cocktail.

Shooters are relative newcomers to the drinks' scene. Invented in the 90s by crafty Canadian barmen to keep out the chill during the long winters, they are attractively layered drinks, consisting of various spirits and liqueurs, poured gently over the back of a spoon into a small shot glass, so that the colors form distinct layers.

Shooters are designed to be swallowed in a single gulp, so that all the flavors meet only in the mouth. They're fun to make and drink, and require a steady hand to keep the layers properly separated.

Blue Lagoon, Harvey Wallbanger, Vodkatini, Salty Dog, Flying Grasshopper and James Bond Cocktail

White Lion

White Lady

Their closest relatives are colorful little concoctions called *pousse-cafés*. These also consist of layers of drinks of different colors, but they're longer drinks, often consisting of four or more layers. Unlike shooters, they are not designed to be downed in a single gulp.

The recipes in this little book should be regarded as guidelines, rather than laws carved in granite. You may find that a small change in the proportions results in a drink closer to your own taste. A Bloody Mary, for example, is basically vodka and tomato juice, but the variations are infinite. Some bartenders add Angostura bitters, others prefer Tabasco. Some add celery salt, while others like plain salt and pepper. One could write a whole book on the local variations of the Bloody Mary around the world.

Be inventive with your cocktails. A good cocktail pleases all the senses. It must look attractive (the selection of glass should show it off to its best advantage, while garnishes add visual appeal), smell good, taste good and even sound good. The tinkling of ice against glass is a very soothing part of the cocktail party.

So raise a pretty glass and drink the old toast: *"Vive le cocktail!"*

Blue Negligee

Love Bite and Green and Gold

SHAKE, STIR OR POUR?

The ingredients of any cocktail should be blended together skilfully to create just the right texture and look. The method used to combine them depends on the nature of the individual ingredients. As a general rule, opaque or cloudy ingredients, such as egg, cream, milk or fruit juices, should be shaken together in a cocktail shaker, usually with a few cubes of ice in it to act as a beater, as well as to cool the mixture and dilute it slightly.

When all the ingredients are clear, the mixture can be stirred in a bar glass, which is like a cylindrical glass jug, usually without a handle, but with calibrations, and a small lip to facilitate pouring.

When separate, distinct layers of color are required, the various ingredients are poured gently into the glass, preferably over a spoon so that they do not disturb the layer below, and should obviously not be stirred or shaken.

These pretty, layered drinks include the fiery little "shooters," designed to be downed in a single gulp to keep out the winter chill.

It takes a skilled and steady-handed cocktail bartender to make a good shooter.

EQUIPMENT

The cocktail bar can be as simply or as elaborately equipped as you please. It does help, however, to have the basic tools of the cocktail trade if you want to take your party seriously.

KNIFE – A sharp knife is essential to good cocktail-creation. It is used to slice lemons, peel oranges and generally trim up the various garnishes that add eye appeal to good cocktails. You'll need a small wooden chopping board with it.

ICE BUCKET – Cocktails are usually served ice-cold, so a plentiful supply of ice is essential. The ice bucket can be of metal, or lined with an insulated material like styrofoam to prevent the ice from melting too fast in hot climates.

ICE TONGS – Tongs are used constantly in the cocktail bar to transfer ice from bucket to shaker, or cocktail glass. It's far more elegant to use ice tongs than to try and fish out ice blocks with a spoon or – worse still – your fingers.

THE MEASURE – Various measures – sometimes called "jiggers" or "tot measures" – are available and

these vary from country to country. For a home cocktail bar you will need two of these, one being twice the capacity of the other.

CORKSCREW – You probably have your own favorite corkscrew already. If not, it pays to spend a little more to get a really good one. It's very messy trying to scoop out the crumbling remains of a cork damaged by an inferior corkscrew. The best corkscrews have spiral screws coated with a non-stick substance to make them slip easily through the cork.

THE SHAKER – Probably the best known of all cocktail equipment is the shaker, which is usually made of silver or stainless steel and consists of three parts – the base, which is a bucket-shaped container, the top, which fits tightly over the base and contains a built-in strainer, and the cap, which closes the shaker and allows it to be shaken vigorously without spilling the contents.

THE MIXING GLASS – This is used for drinks which are stirred and not shaken – generally those with

Ice bucket, ice tongs, strainer, measure, cocktail shaker, bar spoon and opener

clear ingredients. It should
preferably have a lip to facilitate
pouring. It is usually supplied
with a special strainer, sometimes
referred to as a Hawthorn strainer,
with a coil spring all around it,
to enable it to fit snugly into the
top of the mixing glass to hold
back the ice.

THE BAR SPOON – This spoon has a
long, slim handle and a bowl about
the size of a teaspoon and is used
for stirring right down to the
bottom of the mixing glass. Sometimes there is a flat metal disc at the
other end of the spoon, used for
crushing ice, sugar and other solids
at the bottom of the glass.

GLASSES

The glass is essential to the effect of a good cocktail. It should be visually appealing, sparkling clean (polish with a clean cloth) and show off the contents to best effect.

A stemmed glass allows the drinker to hold it without warming the drink, while one with straight sides is best for showing off colors – and layers of color – in particular.

COCKTAIL GLASS – *These elegant glasses, which come in a variety of designs, are often made of cut glass; they usually have stems to prevent the contents being warmed by the drinker's hand, and a bowl with flaring sides.*

PARIS GOBLET – *This is the standard wine glass with a stem and balloon-shaped bowl and is usually used for drinks like pink gin.*

CHAMPAGNE FLUTE – *Sometimes called a "sour" glass, this is a tall, narrow glass with a short stem. It holds sparkling drinks well as the shape retains the bubbles.*

MARTINI GLASS – *Probably the best known of all cocktail glasses, it is often depicted in films and photographs of the cocktail set.*

It has a stem and a simple V-shaped bowl and is used for Martinis and Margaritas.

CHAMPAGNE SAUCER – *Said to have been modelled on the shape of Marie Antoinette's breast, this glass gives a large surface area and allows the bubbles in Champagne to dissipate too fast. However, it is still used for some cocktails.*

BRANDY SNIFTER – *This is a large, balloon-shaped glass with a short stem. The wide balloon allows the aroma of the contents to escape, and the narrow mouth gathers these aromas together to be sniffed and enjoyed.*

LOWBALL GLASS – *A shorter tumbler, sometimes with sloping sides, usually used when serving a Bloody Mary.*

HIGHBALL GLASS – *This is a cylindrical, straight-sided, tall tumbler used for long cocktails like fruit punches and some shooters.*

Top: *Brandy snifter, Lowball, Cocktail, Highball* **Below:** *Martini, Paris goblet, Champagne flute, Champagne saucer*

INGREDIENTS & TRIMMINGS

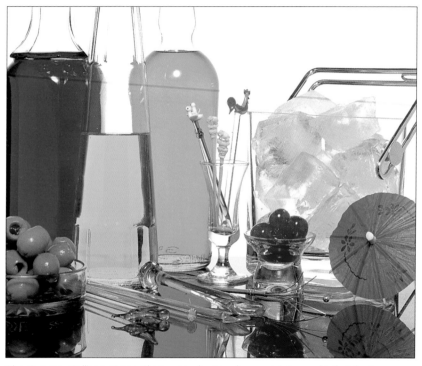

Blue Curaçao, Galliano, Green Chartreuse, shooter glass containing cocktail sticks, ice bucket, umbrella, cherries, swizzle stick, glass stirrers and straw

Most cocktails are based on spirit drinks such as gin, vodka, brandy, whisky or rum, while some use wine, liqueurs or other drinks as their base. Nobody can expect to stock every drink mentioned in this book, but there should be plenty of possibilities within the capacities of your own liquor cabinet.

Good cocktail parties take careful preparation. Try to have all the equipment and ingredients ready in good time, and available where they will be needed.

ICE – Probably most important of all is ice, and more ice. No cocktail is even half complete without a liberal helping of ice, even if it is strained off after mixing. Ice comes in several forms, and serves three main purposes: it chills the drink, dilutes it and acts as a beater when the cocktail is shaken.

The degree of chilling and dilution depends largely on the surface area of the ice being used. Large cubes will chill the drink and act as good beaters, but they will not dilute the drink very much. "Cracked" ice or "crushed" ice presents a large surface area, so it chills and dilutes the drink very quickly. If you do not have an ice crusher in your bar, you can make crushed ice by placing ice cubes in a plastic bag and hammering them with something heavy – a hammer or paper weight, for example. Or you can smack the bag of cubes against a wall, which is undignified, but effective.

Some recipes call for "shaved" ice. This is made in a special machine which, as the name implies, shaves off thin slivers that dissolve quite quickly, and create a sort of icy slush. A similar effect is obtained by placing crushed ice in a blender with the cocktail ingredients and blending them together for a few seconds. Never put whole ice cubes in a blender. They could seriously damage it.

All the recipes in this book indicate the best way to use your ice for that particular drink.

OTHER INGREDIENTS – Eggs are used in several drinks, as are fruit juices, cream, Angostura bitters, Worcestershire sauce, super fine sugar, honey, sugar syrup and iced tea.

It is always a good idea to have a few brightly colored drinks, like Crème de Menthe and Blue Curaçao to add an exotic touch.

Mixers range from tomato juice, ginger ale, soda water and lemonade to grenadine, which is a red, non-alcoholic syrup made from pomegranates.

FROSTINGS – Cocktail glasses are sometimes frosted, to add an element of surprise, a different texture and additional flavor.

To frost the rim of a glass, first dip it into a saucer of egg white or lemon juice, then dip the wet rim into fine sugar (or salt in the case of a Margarita). Tidy up any ragged edges of the frosting if necessary.

GARNISHES – These are important, both for flavor and appearance. They should always be crisp and fresh. Lemon is probably the most common garnish, either used as a thin slice, cut to slip over the rim of the glass, or as a twist, a coiled sliver of lemon rind in the drink.

Cherries add a colorful dash of red, and olives give a savory tang. Some recipes suggest a slice of cucumber as garnish. Other popular garnishes include mint leaves, slices of kiwi fruit, strawberries, pineapple chunks, oranges (and orange rind).

DECORATIONS – Swizzle sticks are pretty, and also handy for stirring the cocktail. Drinks that contain chunks of fruit can be given a tropical look by adding a little paper parasol. Pretty plastic straws can also brighten up a cocktail and add to the fun. Cocktail sticks are useful for holding garnishes, and also for fishing interesting pieces of fruit or olives from the bottom of the glass.

SYRUP – Cocktail recipes sometimes call for "gomme" syrup, or sugar syrup. This is a non-alcoholic sweetening syrup, and if you do not have it in your bar, here's an easy recipe to make your own:

Place two cups of granulated sugar in a saucepan and add a cup of water. Heat gently, stirring all the time, until the sugar is all dissolved. Allow it to cool, and then bottle it for cocktail use.

THE MEASURES

Some cocktail recipes give measures in fluid ounces while others prefer millilitres. Some even refer to measures as a "six-out" or a "three-out," containing five-sixths of a fluid ounce and one and two thirds of a fluid ounce respectively.

The American "jigger" contains one and a half fluid ounces, and sometimes has a smaller measure, called a "pony," attached to the bottom. The pony contains one fluid ounce.

To make matters even more confusing, British fluid ounces are different to American fluid ounces.

The good news is that the actual capacity of the measure is not important. What is important is to get the PROPORTIONS of the drink correct. This is why we use the term "parts" in this little guide. "One part of gin to two parts of vermouth" will taste the same whether the "parts" are teaspoons or buckets.

When mixing the cocktails in this book, use your regular bar measure (whether it's a British measure or an American one) as "one part" when mixing a cocktail for one person. It probably holds about 50 ml, or 1½ fluid ounces.

If you're mixing for more than one person, use whatever measure seems appropriate – a wine glass, perhaps, or a coffee mug, depending on numbers.

Cocktail shakers, decorations for glasses and Angostura bitters pouring bottle

RUM COCKTAILS

Rum makes a romantic base for any cocktail, evoking thoughts of tropical islands and the schooners on the Caribbean. Many rum cocktails appropriately include tropical fruit or fruit juices. These recipes use either dark rum or light, white rum such as Bacardi.

PLANTERS' PUNCH

Almost every bartender has his own version of this refreshing drink. Some add sugar while others like a dash of Maraschino in the mixture. Here's a basic recipe to use as the starting point for your own version.

One part dark rum

Two parts fresh orange juice

Juice of half a fresh lime or lemon

One teaspoon superfine sugar per glass

A dash of grenadine or gomme syrup per glass

A cocktail cherry

Crushed ice

◆ Place about a cup of crushed ice in a cocktail shaker.
◆ Add the rum, orange juice, lime or lemon juice, sugar and grenadine or gomme syrup.
◆ Shake very well and strain into a chilled lowball glass.
◆ Serve decorated with the cocktail cherry on a stick.

Planters' Punch

BLACK DEVIL

Four parts dark rum

One part Italian vermouth

A black olive

Ice cubes

◆ Place four cubes of ice in a bar glass, add the rum and vermouth and stir well.
◆ Strain into a cocktail glass and serve with a black olive.

White Lion and Black Devil

WHITE LION

Three parts light rum

One part lemon juice

Half a teaspoon of grenadine per glass

A teaspoon of sugar (or to taste) per glass

A dash of Angostura bitters per glass

Ice cubes

◆ Place five ice cubes in a cocktail shaker and add all ingredients.
◆ Shake well, then strain into a chilled cocktail glass and serve.

MAI TAI

Here's another popular tropical cooler for a summer evening.

Two parts light rum

One part Curaçao

One part sugar syrup

One part fresh lime juice

Two parts grenadine

Half a teaspoon of sugar per glass

A slice of pineapple

A cocktail cherry

Ice cubes

◆ Place five ice cubes in a cocktail shaker and add the rum, Curaçao, sugar syrup, lime juice, grenadine and sugar.
◆ Shake well, then strain over ice cubes in a large cocktail glass.
◆ Decorate with the pineapple slice and cherry.

Mai Tai

21

BRASS MONKEY

As with many rum-based drinks, this one originated at sea, where the "brass monkey" was the metal rack on which cannon balls were stored. If it became very cold, the rack contracted and the cannon balls fell off, hence the famous saying: "Cold enough to freeze the balls off a brass monkey". There's nothing rude about it. This drink should help to keep the monkey warm.

One part light rum

One part vodka

Four parts orange juice

A slice of orange

Ice cubes

◆ Fill a highball glass with cubes of ice and pour in the rum, vodka and orange juice.
◆ Stir carefully, then serve decorated with the slice of orange, and a straw.

Brass Monkey and Zombie

ZOMBIE

The zombie is one of those drinks that takes a good deal of preparation. In American specialist cocktail bars they use an especially large glass for it. It's known, of course, as a "Zombie Glass".

Two parts light rum

One part dark rum

One part Curaçao

One part lemon juice

One part orange juice

One part pineapple juice

Half a part of guava or papaya juice

One teaspoon of Pernod per glass

Half a part of sugar syrup

Mint leaves

A stick of pineapple

Crushed ice

◆ Place about half a cup of crushed ice in a cocktail shaker and add all the ingredients except the mint and pineapple.
◆ Shake very well and strain into a tall glass (or zombie glass, if you have one).
◆ Decorate with the mint leaves and stick of pineapple and serve.

CHOCOLATE RUM

One part light rum

Two teaspoons of Crème de Cacao per glass

Two teaspoons of white Crème de Menthe per glass

Two teaspoons of thick cream per glass

One teaspoon of heavy, dark rum per glass

Ice cubes

◆ Place five cubes of ice in a cocktail shaker, add the white rum, Crème de Cacao, Crème de Menthe and thick cream.
◆ Shake well, then strain into a lowball glass filled with ice cubes.
◆ Finally, trickle the dark rum over the top and serve.

Chocolate Rum

SHARK'S TOOTH

Surfers know a shark's tooth brings luck. Here's a happy drink to enjoy after catching a few good waves.

Three parts dark rum

One part lemon juice

One part lime juice

Half a part grenadine

Soda water

A slice of lemon

Ice cubes

◆ Place six ice cubes in a cocktail shaker and add the rum, lemon juice, lime juice and grenadine.
◆ Shake well, then strain the mixture into a highball glass filled with ice cubes.
◆ Top off with soda water and decorate with a slice of lemon.

Shark's Tooth

GROG

The original navy grog was simply diluted rum. Very boring. Navy Grog on page 33 and this recipe are distinct improvements.

Two parts dark rum

One sugar cube

Three whole cloves

One cinnamon stick

Boiling water

A twist of lemon

◆ Place the rum, sugar cube, cloves and cinnamon in a mug (no sissy cocktail glasses for sailors!).
◆ Add boiling water to fill the mug.
◆ Stir until the sugar is dissolved.
◆ Decorate with a twist of lemon.

CUBA LIBRE

In spite of its fancy name, this is probably the popular drink referred to in the old song: "Rum and Coca-Cola". It's been around for some time.

One part light rum

Six parts cola

Half a fresh lime

Ice cubes

◆ Pour the rum into a highball glass, add the cola and two ice cubes and stir gently.
◆ Squeeze the juice of half a fresh lime over it and serve.

CORKSCREW

Three parts light rum

One part dry vermouth

One part peach liqueur

A slice of lime

Ice cubes

◆ Place four ice cubes in a cocktail shaker, add the rum, vermouth and peach liqueur and shake well.
◆ Strain into a chilled cocktail glass and decorate with a slice of lime.

Corkscrew, Cuba Libre and Grog

PINA COLADA

One part light rum

One part coconut cream

Two parts pineapple juice

A slice of pineapple

A cocktail cherry

Crushed ice

◆ Place three tablespoons of crushed ice in a cocktail shaker, add the rum, coconut cream and pineapple juice and shake well.
◆ Strain into a highball glass and decorate with the fruit.

BLOSSOM

One part light rum

One part fresh orange juice

A dash of grenadine per glass

Ice cubes

◆ Place five cubes of ice in a cocktail shaker.
◆ Add the rum, orange juice and dash of grenadine and shake well.
◆ Strain into a cocktail glass and serve undecorated.

Blossom and Pina Colada

BEE'S KNEES

This is a survivor of the old speakeasy days during the Prohibition era.

Two parts light rum

One part fresh orange juice

One part fresh lime juice

A teaspoon of honey (or sugar) per glass

Two dashes of orange bitters per glass

Orange rind

Ice cubes

◆ Place four cubes of ice in a cocktail shaker and add the rum, orange juice, lime juice, honey or sugar and bitters.

◆ Shake well, then strain into a chilled cocktail glass.

◆ Twist the orange rind above the glass to add a whiff of citrus oil, then drop the rind into the glass and serve.

Bee's Knees

DAIQUIRI

The daiquiri was apparently named after a nickel mine of that name in Cuba, where American engineers were unable to obtain their favorite whiskey, and so invented a drink using local rum.

There are many variations of this old favorite, all based on white rum and lime juice. Some cocktail makers add obscure syrups and other ingredients. Sometimes grapefruit juice is combined with the lime juice and sometimes gomme syrup is used instead of sugar, but this is one of the simpler recipes.

One part light rum

The juice of half a lime

Half a teaspoon of sugar per glass

A slice of lime

A cocktail cherry

Ice cubes

◆ Place four or five ice cubes in a cocktail shaker, combine the lime juice and sugar and add it to the shaker together with the rum.
◆ Shake very well, then strain into a cocktail glass.
◆ Decorate with the slice of lime and cocktail cherry spiked together on a cocktail stick.

DAIQUIRI BLOSSOM

Here's a variation on the daiquiri theme for those who like things a little sweeter.

One part light rum

One part fresh orange juice

A dash of Maraschino per glass

A slice of orange

A cocktail cherry

Ice cubes

◆ Place four ice cubes in a cocktail shaker, add the rum and orange juice and a dash of Maraschino.
◆ Shake well, then strain into a cocktail glass.
◆ Decorate with the slice of orange and cherry speared together on a cocktail stick.

Daiquiri and Daiquiri Blossom

WATERMELON COOLER

Half a cup diced fresh watermelon, deseeded

Two parts white rum

A splash of lime juice

A tablespoon of Maraschino per glass

A teaspoon of superfine sugar per glass

A slice of lime

Crushed ice and ice cubes

◆ Place the watermelon, rum, lime juice, Maraschino, fine sugar and half a cup of crushed ice into a blender and blend for approximately 10 seconds.
◆ Pour into a highball glass, and when the foam subsides, add ice cubes to fill the glass.
◆ Serve decorated with a slice of lime.

Navy Grog and Watermelon Cooler

NAVY GROG

The original Navy grog was just rum diluted with water. Later, the British Royal Navy introduced lime juice into the sailors' diet, creating a nation of Limeys, and I'm sure that even those old matelots would have approved of this fine drink.

Two parts dark rum

One part light rum

One part lime juice

One part orange juice

One part pineapple juice

One part guava nectar

A teaspoon of Falernum per glass

Mint leaves

Crushed ice

◆ Place half a cup of crushed ice in a blender, add the two rums and all the fruit juices, plus the teaspoon (or a little more to taste) of Falernum (a syrup with ginger and lime flavors).
◆ Blend for ten seconds at high speed, then strain the mixture into a highball glass.
◆ Crush the mint leaves slightly to release their aroma and float several on the surface of the cocktail.
◆ Serve with a straw.

BRANDY COCKTAILS

Brandy is a warm, golden liquor that makes splendid cocktails for chilly winter evenings. Although cognac is considered the "champagne" of brandies, it is probably a waste to mix it in cocktails. Most wine-producing countries make brandy that is quite acceptable, so try one of these instead.

B AND B

One part brandy

One part Bénédictine

A twist of lime

Ice cubes

◆ Place two or three ice cubes in a bar glass and add the brandy and Bénédictine.
◆ Stir and strain into a small cocktail glass.
◆ Decorate with the twist of lime.

BRANDY ALEXANDER

One part brandy

One part Crème de Cacao

One part cream

Ice cubes

◆ Place four ice cubes in a cocktail shaker, add all the ingredients and shake well.
◆ Strain into a chilled cocktail glass and serve undecorated.

Brandy Alexander and B and B

BLACKSMITH COCKTAIL

The English drink called simply a "blacksmith" consists of half a pint of Guinness stout and half a pint of barley wine. The Blacksmith Cocktail, however, is slightly more complicated.

One part brandy

One part Drambuie

One part Crème de Café

Ice cubes

◆ Place four ice cubes in a bar glass and add the brandy, Drambuie and Crème de Café.

◆ Stir well and serve on the rocks in a lowball glass.

Blacksmith Cocktail

BRANDY COCKTAIL

There are many cocktails called simply "Brandy Cocktail". Here's a standard recipe to try.

One part brandy

One part dry vermouth

A dash of Angostura bitters per glass

Lemon rind

A cocktail cherry

Ice cubes

◆ Place four or five cubes of ice in a bar glass and add the brandy, vermouth and a dash of bitters.
◆ Strain into a cocktail glass and add a squeeze of lemon juice from the rind.
◆ Decorate with a cherry on a cocktail stick.

Brandy Cocktail

JUMBO

Use a small measure for this cocktail, as there are quite a few ingredients. Or you can use a normal measure and pour more than one drink. That's even better.

One part brandy

One part Italian vermouth

One part French vermouth

A dash of Campari per glass

A dash of Pernod per glass

Ice cubes

◆ Place four ice cubes in a cocktail shaker, add the brandy, both vermouths, Campari and Pernod, and shake well.
◆ Strain into a cocktail glass and serve undecorated.

Jumbo

SIDECAR

One part brandy

One part Cointreau

One part lemon juice

A slice of orange

A cocktail cherry

Crushed ice

◆ Half fill a cocktail shaker with crushed ice. Add the liquid ingredients, shake well and strain into a chilled cocktail glass.
◆ Decorate with the slice of orange and cocktail cherry.

HORSE'S NECK

One part brandy

Ginger ale

A spiral of lemon rind

Ice cubes

◆ Place two ice cubes in a highball glass and add the brandy.
◆ Decorate with the spiral of lemon rind and top off with ginger ale to taste.

Horse's Neck and Sidecar

BRANDY SOUR

Four parts brandy

One part lemon juice

One part orange juice

Sugar

A slice of lemon

Ice cubes

◆ Place six cubes of ice in a cocktail shaker and pour in the brandy, lemon juice and orange juice.
◆ Add sugar to taste – half a teaspoon to a teaspoon per glass is usually enough.
◆ Shake well and strain into a cocktail glass.
◆ Decorate with a slice of lemon.

STINGER

Two parts brandy

One part white Crème de Menthe

Ice cubes

◆ Place six ice cubes in a cocktail shaker and add the brandy and Crème de Menthe.
◆ Shake well, then strain into a cocktail glass.
◆ Serve undecorated.

PRAIRIE OYSTER

This is reputed to be a great cure for a hangover. The author takes no responsibility for its effects.

One egg yolk

One part brandy

Worcestershire sauce

Cayenne pepper

Tabasco sauce

Celery salt

◆ Place the unbroken yolk carefully in a cocktail glass.
◆ Add the brandy, several dashes of Worcestershire sauce, a pinch of cayenne pepper, a dash of Tabasco and a pinch of celery salt.
◆ Do not mix at all.
◆ The right way to consume this concoction is to close your eyes, take a deep breath and swallow it all in a single gulp. Oops!

Brandy Sour, Prairie Oyster and Stinger

GRENADIER

One part brandy (usually Cognac)

One part ginger brandy

A dash of Jamaican ginger per glass

A teaspoon of sugar per glass

Ice cubes

◆ Place five ice cubes in a cocktail shaker and add all the ingredients.
◆ Shake well and strain into a cocktail glass.
◆ Serve undecorated.

BETWEEN THE SHEETS

One part brandy

One part white rum

One part Cointreau

A teaspoon of lemon juice per glass

Lemon rind

Ice cubes

◆ Place eight ice cubes in a cocktail shaker and add all the ingredients, except the lemon rind.
◆ Shake well and strain into a cocktail glass.
◆ Serve decorated with a twist of lemon rind.

BRANDY MANHATTAN

Four parts brandy

One part sweet vermouth

A dash of Angostura bitters per glass

A maraschino cherry

Ice cubes

◆ Place four ice cubes in a bar glass, add the brandy, vermouth and a dash of bitters.
◆ Stir well, then strain into a chilled cocktail glass.
◆ Decorate with the maraschino cherry on a cocktail stick.

Clockwise from left: *Grenadier, Between the Sheets and Brandy Manhattan*

TANTALUS

One part brandy

One part lemon juice

One part passion fruit juice

Ice cubes

◆ Place four cubes of ice in a cocktail shaker, add all the ingredients and shake well.
◆ Strain into a cocktail glass and serve undecorated.

Tantalus and Picasso

PICASSO

Three parts brandy

One part Dubonnet rouge

One part lime juice

A teaspoon of sugar per glass

Orange rind

Ice cubes

◆ Place four cubes of ice in a cocktail shaker, add the brandy, Dubonnet, lime juice and sugar.
◆ Shake well, then strain into a chilled cocktail glass and decorate with a twist of orange rind.

COFFEE

Nobody seems quite sure why this cocktail is called "coffee" but it appears in various forms in many of the standard reference works on cocktails. The only coffee thing about it is the coffee beans usually used as decoration.

One part brandy

Two parts port

An egg yolk

A dash of Curaçao per glass

A teaspoon of sugar per glass

Coffee beans

Ice cubes

◆ Place five cubes of ice in a cocktail shaker.
◆ Add the brandy, port, Curaçao, egg yolk and sugar.
◆ Shake well, then strain into a lowball glass.
◆ Float a few roasted coffee beans on top.

Coffee

BULL'S MILK

Here's a good nightcap for
a cowboy.

One part brandy

Sugar syrup

A cup of milk

Grated nutmeg

Ground cinnamon

Ice cubes

◆ Place four ice cubes in a cocktail
shaker, add the brandy, milk and
sugar syrup to taste.
◆ Shake well and strain into a
highball glass. Sprinkle nutmeg
and cinnamon over the top.

PHOEBE SNOW

One part brandy

One part Dubonnet rouge

A dash of Pernod per glass

Crushed ice

◆ Place a few scoops of crushed
ice in a cocktail shaker, add the
brandy, Dubonnet and dash of
Pernod and shake well.
◆ Strain into a chilled cocktail
glass and serve undecorated.

VARIATION

This drink can also be mixed in a
blender, using slightly less crushed
ice. The result looks more like the
snow in its name.

MIKADO

A generous part of brandy

Two dashes of Angostura bitters

Two dashes of orgeat

Two dashes of Curaçao

Two dashes of Creme de noyaux

A cocktail cherry

Lemon rind

Ice cubes

◆ Place six ice cubes in a bar
glass, add the brandy and dashes
of orgeat (an almond-flavored
syrup), Curaçao and noyaux
(a French liqueur made from
peach and apricot kernels).
◆ Stir together until well blended.
◆ Strain into a cocktail glass, add
the cherry and a squeeze of lemon
rind juice.
◆ Serve decorated with a small
paper parasol.

Phoebe Snow, Bull's Milk and Mikado

46

CLASSIC

Two parts brandy

Half a part lemon juice

Half a part Curaçao

Half a part Maraschino

Lemon juice

Superfine sugar

A twist of lemon rind

Ice cubes

◆ Place three or four ice cubes in a bar glass and pour in the brandy, lemon juice, Curaçao and Maraschino.
◆ Stir well.
◆ Frost the rim of a cocktail glass by dipping it first into lemon juice and then into the sugar.
◆ Pour in the cocktail and decorate with a twist of lemon rind.

Classic

48

HARVARD
(Obviously this one originated at the famous American university.)

One part brandy

Half a teaspoon of sugar per glass

One part sweet vermouth

A dash of Angostura bitters per glass

A slice of lemon

Ice cubes

◆ Place four ice cubes in a cocktail shaker and add the brandy, sugar and sweet vermouth.
◆ Shake well.
◆ Splash a dash of bitters into a cocktail glass and swirl it around to coat the sides evenly.
◆ Strain the cocktail from the shaker into the glass and decorate with a slice of lemon.

Harvard

GIN COCKTAILS

*Gin forms the basis of many famous cocktails,
and the most famous of them all is
undoubtedly the Martini, in its various forms.
Other well-known gin-based cocktails are
White Lady, Bronx, John Collins and Gin Sling.*

GIN SLING

The gin sling is one of the classics and, like many of the old favorites, comes in a variety of styles. Here's a recipe that should please most palates.

Two parts gin

One part fresh lemon juice

Half a part of gomme or sugar syrup

Soda water

Crushed ice

◆ Place about three tablespoons of crushed ice in a lowball glass. Add the gin, lemon juice and gomme or sugar syrup.
◆ Top off with soda water, stir gently and serve.

Gin Sling

WHITE LADY

There are several versions of this elegant little drink, some use vodka as a base, but gin is the most popular starting point.

One part gin

Half a part Cointreau

Half a part lemon juice

Half an egg white

Ice cubes

◆ Place the gin, Cointreau, lemon juice and egg white in a cocktail shaker with four ice cubes.
◆ Shake very well, then strain into a cocktail glass. Serve undecorated.

GIN FIZZ

You can hardly imagine a cocktail simpler than this.

One part gin

One teaspoon of sugar per glass

Soda water

A cocktail cherry

Ice cubes

◆ Place the sugar in the bottom of a lowball glass, add the gin and two ice cubes and stir until the sugar has dissolved.
◆ Pour soda water over the mixture to fill the glass and stir gently.
◆ Decorate with the cocktail cherry on a stick.

NEGRONI

This is a simple and delicious classic among cocktails.

One part gin

One part sweet vermouth

One part Campari

Lemon rind

Crushed ice

◆ Place half a cup of crushed ice in a cocktail shaker, add the gin, vermouth and Campari.
◆ Shake well, then strain into a cocktail glass. Twist a strip of lemon rind over it to add zest, then drop the rind into the drink and serve.

White Lady, Gin Fizz and Negroni

THE MARTINI

Probably the best known of all cocktails, the martini comes in a thousand different guises. Ratios of gin to vermouth vary infinitely and in some circles it is considered very fashionable to have as little vermouth as possible. Legend has it that one New York barman used to put neat gin into a cocktail glass, take a mouthful of vermouth and whisper the word "vermouth" over the glass!

The quantities given here are obviously only guidelines.

DRY MARTINI

One part gin

One part dry vermouth

A green olive

Ice cubes

◆ Place four ice cubes in a bar mixing glass and add the gin and dry vermouth.
◆ Stir well, then strain into a martini glass to remove the ice.
◆ Decorate with the olive on a cocktail stick.

SWEET MARTINI

One part gin

One part sweet vermouth

A cocktail cherry

Ice cubes

◆ Place eight cubes of ice in a mixing glass and add the gin and sweet vermouth.
◆ Stir well, then strain into a martini glass to remove the ice.
◆ Decorate with a cocktail cherry.

Medium Martini,
Sweet Martini and Dry Martini

MEDIUM MARTINI

This cocktail is usually served undecorated.

One part gin

One part dry vermouth

One part sweet vermouth

Ice cubes

◆ Place eight ice cubes in a mixing glass, add the gin, dry vermouth and sweet vermouth.
◆ Stir well, then strain into a martini glass to remove the ice.

GIN DAIQUIRI

Here's a pleasing variation on the Daiquiri theme.

Three parts dry gin

One part light rum

One part lime juice

A teaspoon of sugar per glass

Ice cubes

◆ Place four ice cubes in a cocktail shaker and add all the ingredients.
◆ Shake well, then strain into a chilled cocktail glass.

GIN ALEXANDER

One part gin

One part Crème de Cacao

One part cream

Ice cubes

◆ Place four ice cubes in a cocktail shaker, add the gin, Crème de Cacao and cream.
◆ Shake well, then strain into a chilled cocktail glass.

Gin Daiquiri and Gin Alexander

BLUE DEVIL

Three parts gin

One part Blue Curaçao

One part lemon juice

A slice of lemon

Ice cubes

◆ Place five ice cubes in a cocktail shaker, add the gin, Blue Curaçao and lemon juice and shake well.
◆ Strain into a cocktail glass and decorate with the slice of lemon.

Blue Devil and Banana Cocktail

BANANA COCKTAIL

One part gin

One part light rum

Two parts Crème de Banane

A slice of kiwi fruit

Ice cubes

◆ Place four ice cubes in a cocktail shaker, add the gin, light rum and Crème de Banane and shake well.
◆ Strain into a cocktail glass.
◆ Decorate with the kiwi fruit.

JOURNALIST

I have no idea at all why this drink is called a journalist. It was probably invented by some weary reporter on night shift.

Two parts dry gin

One part Italian vermouth

One part French vermouth

Two dashes of lemon juice per glass

Two dashes of Triple Sec per glass

A dash of Angostura bitters per glass

Ice cubes

◆ Place five ice cubes in a cocktail shaker and add all the ingredients.
◆ Shake very well, then strain into a cocktail glass.
◆ Serve undecorated.

BRONX

This is a relic of the old American Prohibition era and was originally made with "bathtub gin" of very dubious quality. Fine dry gin certainly improves it. It can be made drier or sweeter by varying the proportions of the dry and sweet vermouth.

Three parts dry gin

One part orange juice

Half a part dry vermouth

Half a part sweet vermouth

Ice cubes

◆ Place four ice cubes in a cocktail shaker, add the gin, orange juice and vermouth and shake well.
◆ Strain into a cocktail glass and serve undecorated.

Journalist and Bronx

ZUMBO

Three parts dry gin

One part Grand Marnier

One part Italian vermouth

A dash of Campari per glass

Ice cubes

◆ Place four ice cubes in a cocktail shaker, add the gin, Grand Marnier, vermouth and dash of Campari.
◆ Shake well and strain into a cocktail glass.
◆ Serve undecorated.

SILVER BULLET

Two parts gin

One part kümmel

One part lemon juice

Ice cubes

◆ Place the gin, kümmel and lemon juice in a cocktail shaker with six cubes of ice.
◆ Shake well, then strain into a cocktail glass.
◆ Serve undecorated.

GIN AND LIME

There are certainly plenty of variations on this theme! Many bartenders merely add a splash of lime juice to the gin and top off with water or soda. Very boring! Try this very English version.

Three parts gin

One part fresh lime juice

One part fresh orange juice

A teaspoon of Roses lime juice cordial per glass

A twist of lime or lemon rind

Ice cubes

◆ Place four ice cubes in a cocktail shaker and add the gin, lime juice, orange juice and lime juice cordial.
◆ Shake well, then strain into a chilled cocktail glass.
◆ Squeeze the lemon or lime rind over it to add fragrance, the serve decorated with the twist of lime or lemon rind.

Silver Bullet, Gin and Lime and Zumbo

60

JOHN COLLINS

Two parts dry gin

One part lemon juice

*A teaspoon of gomme syrup
(or honey, or even a teaspoon
of sugar) per glass*

Soda water

A slice of lemon

A sprig of mint

Ice cubes

◆ Place six ice cubes in a
cocktail shaker, pour in the
gin, lemon juice and syrup.
◆ Shake well, then strain into
a chilled highball glass.
◆ Top off the glass with soda
water and stir gently.
◆ Decorate with a slice of lemon
and a sprig of mint.

John Collins

GREEN DEVIL

It seems there are all colors of devils in the cocktail cabinet. You'll find recipes for a black devil and a blue devil in this book, as well as this green one.

Three parts gin

One part lime juice

Half a part green Crème de Menthe

Two sprigs of mint

Ice cubes

◆ Place four ice cubes in a bar glass, add the gin, lime juice and Crème de Menthe.
◆ Stir well, then strain into a chilled cocktail glass.
◆ Lightly crush the mint leaves to release their aroma, then drop them into the drink.

Green Devil

BLUE ARROW

Two parts gin

One part Cointreau

One part lime juice

One part Blue Curaçao

Crushed ice

◆ Half fill a cocktail shaker with crushed ice.
◆ Pour in the gin, Cointreau, lime juice and Blue Curaçao and shake well for five seconds.
◆ Strain into a chilled cocktail glass and serve undecorated.

PINK GIN

The pink gin is a frightfully British drink, but the Americans have adapted it to their own cocktail style. It's the drink that kept Sir Francis Chichester cheerful on his long solo voyage around the world.
  The British simply put two dashes of Angostura bitters into a glass and add neat gin. The Americans do a little more.

Two parts dry gin

Angostura bitters

Ice cubes

◆ Place four ice cubes in a bar glass and add two dashes of Angostura bitters.
◆ Pour in the gin and stir well.
◆ Strain into a chilled cocktail glass.

Blue Arrow and Pink Gin

GIMLET

This is one of the classics that appears in various forms all over the world.

Two parts gin

One part lime juice cordial

A slice of lime

Crushed ice .

◆ Place three tablespoons of crushed ice in a cocktail shaker.
◆ Add the gin and lime juice and shake well.
◆ Strain into a cocktail glass.
◆ Decorate with a slice of lime and serve with a pretty straw.

VARIATION
Sometimes this cocktail is given a splash of soda water and served in a lowball glass.

PINK LADY

This is an attractive little drink that tastes as wonderful as it looks.

Two parts gin

One part lime juice

A teaspoon of cream per glass

Half an egg white per glass

A teaspoon of grenadine per glass

Sugar

Ice cubes

◆ Place four cubes of ice in a cocktail shaker, add the gin, lime juice, cream and egg white.
◆ Shake thoroughly.
◆ Moisten the rim of a chilled cocktail glass with grenadine and frost it with sugar.
◆ Strain the cocktail into the frosted glass.

Gimlet and Pink Lady

VODKA COCKTAILS

Vodka is the ideal cocktail spirit, adding alcoholic bite without changing the flavor too drastically. It's also low in the components which cause hangovers, and, because it's almost flavorless, it leaves no tell-tale signs on the breath!

BARBARA COCKTAIL

One part vodka

Half a part Crème de Cacao

Half a part cream

Ice cubes

◆ Place four ice cubes in a cocktail shaker and add the vodka, Crème de Cacao and cream.
◆ Shake well, then strain into a cocktail glass. Serve undecorated.

BLACK RUSSIAN

Two parts vodka

One part Kahlúa or any coffee liqueur

Ice cubes

◆ Place a few ice cubes in a cocktail shaker, add the ingredients and shake well.
◆ Place several ice cubes in a lowball glass and strain the contents of the shaker over them.

Black Russian and Barbara Cocktail

69

VODKATINI

As the name suggests, this is a martini variation, using vodka instead of gin.

Two parts vodka

One part dry vermouth

A twist of lemon rind

Ice cubes

◆ In a mixing glass place four cubes of ice.
◆ Add the vodka and vermouth and stir well.
◆ Strain the mixture into a cocktail glass, add a twist of lemon rind juice, then decorate with the lemon twist.

BANANA PUNCH

One part vodka

Two–thirds of a part apricot brandy

The juice of half a lime

Soda water

Sliced banana

A sprig of mint

Crushed ice

◆ Mix the vodka, apricot brandy and lime juice in a bar glass.
◆ Fill a highball glass two-thirds with crushed ice.
◆ Pour the ingredients over the ice and top off with soda water.
◆ Decorate with slices of banana and a sprig of mint.

BLUE LAGOON

Blue drinks always add an exotic touch to a party. This one is no exception.

Three parts vodka

One part Blue Curaçao

Three parts pineapple juice

Three dashes of green Chartreuse per glass

A slice of pineapple

Crushed ice

◆ Place half a cup of crushed ice in a cocktail shaker and add the vodka, Blue Curaçao, pineapple juice and green Chartreuse.
◆ Shake well and strain into a lowball glass.
◆ Serve decorated with the slice of pineapple.

Vodkatini, Blue Lagoon and Banana Punch

BLOODY MARY

There are many variations of this old favorite. Vary the ingredients to suit your own palate. The South American version of the Bloody Mary is called a Bloody Maria, and is the same basic recipe, using tequila instead of vodka.

Two parts vodka

Six parts tomato juice

A teaspoon of ketchup per glass

A dash of Worcestershire sauce per glass

A pinch of celery salt per glass

A dash of Tabasco sauce per glass

A thin stick of celery

Ice cubes

◆ Place four ice cubes in a cocktail shaker and add the vodka and tomato juice.
◆ Add the ketchup, a dash each of Worcestershire sauce and Tabasco and a pinch of celery salt.
◆ Shake well, strain into a highball glass and serve with the celery.

BULLSHOT

This is reputed to be a fast cure for a hangover. Or perhaps a fast cause for one!

One part vodka

Two and a half parts cold clear beef bouillon

A dash of lemon juice per glass

A dash of Worcestershire sauce per glass

A pinch of celery salt per glass

Ice cubes

◆ Place five or six ice cubes in a bar glass and add the vodka and beef bouillon.
◆ Add a dash each of lemon juice and Worcestershire sauce and a pinch of celery salt.
◆ Stir well, then strain over ice cubes in a lowball glass.

Bloody Mary and Bullshot

HARVEY WALLBANGER

One part vodka

Two parts orange juice

Two teaspoons of Galliano per glass

A slice of orange

Ice cubes

◆ Place five ice cubes in a cocktail shaker, add the vodka and orange juice and shake well.
◆ Strain into a highball glass and add two cubes of ice.
◆ Float two teaspoons of Galliano on the top and decorate with a slice of orange.
◆ Serve with a straw.

Harvey Wallbanger

JAMES BOND COCKTAIL

Only the smooth-tongued Double-oh-seven could have thought up a cocktail as deliciously decadent as this one. Of course the Champagne has to be Dom Perignon and, please, no uncouth shaking or stirring with this one.

A cube of sugar per glass

Angostura bitters

One part vodka

Chilled Champagne

Crushed ice

A twist of lemon rind

◆ Soak the cube of sugar in Angostura bitters and place it gently in the bottom of a chilled Champagne flute.
◆ Add a spoonful of crushed ice and the vodka and top off gently with Champagne.
◆ Decorate with the spiral of lemon rind.

James Bond Cocktail

WHITE RUSSIAN

Two parts vodka

One part Crème de Cacao

One part cream

Ice cubes

◆ Place four ice cubes in a cocktail shaker and add the remaining ingredients.
◆ Shake very well, then strain into a chilled cocktail glass.
◆ Serve undecorated.

SCREWDRIVER

One part vodka

Three parts freshly squeezed orange juice

A teaspoon of lemon juice per glass

Crushed ice

◆ Place about a cup of crushed ice in a cocktail shaker.
◆ Add the vodka, orange juice and lemon juice and shake very well.
◆ Strain into a chilled lowball glass.

SALTY DOG
Here's a good drink for a sailor.

Four parts vodka

One part fresh grapefruit juice

A teaspoon of lemon juice per glass

Ice cubes

Salt

◆ Place four ice cubes in a cocktail shaker and add the vodka, grapefruit juice and lemon juice.
◆ Shake well, then strain into a well-chilled cocktail glass.
◆ Sprinkle with a liberal helping of salt and serve.

FLYING GRASSHOPPER

Two parts vodka

One part green Crème de Menthe

One part white Crème de Cacao

Ice cubes

◆ Place four cubes of ice in a bar glass and add all the ingredients.
◆ Stir well, then strain into a chilled cocktail glass.
◆ Serve undecorated.

White Russian, Salty Dog, Flying Grasshopper and Screwdriver

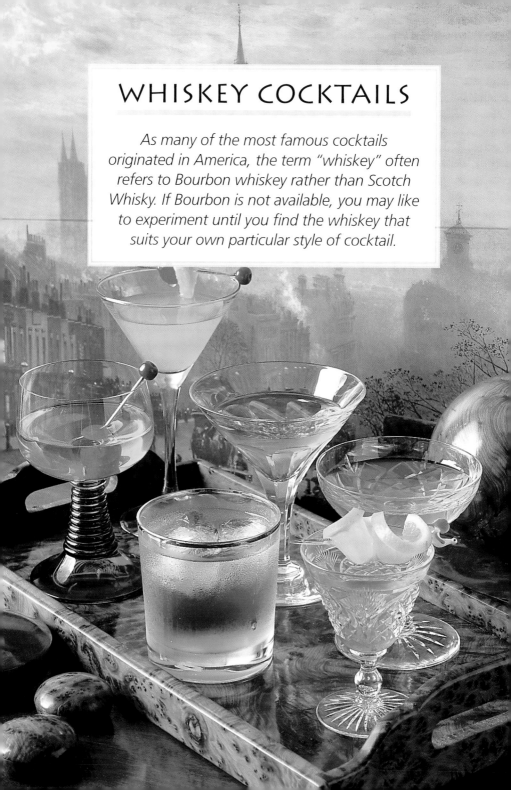

WHISKEY COCKTAILS

As many of the most famous cocktails originated in America, the term "whiskey" often refers to Bourbon whiskey rather than Scotch Whisky. If Bourbon is not available, you may like to experiment until you find the whiskey that suits your own particular style of cocktail.

THREE RIVERS

This one originates in Canada, so perfectionists may like to use Canadian whiskey for a dash of authenticity.

Two parts Canadian whiskey (well, any whiskey will do)

One part Dubonnet

One part Triple Sec

Ice cubes

◆ Place five or six ice cubes in a cocktail shaker and add the whiskey, Dubonnet and Triple Sec.
◆ Shake well, then strain into a chilled lowball glass filled with ice cubes.
◆ Serve undecorated.

Three Rivers

WHISKEY SOUR

This is an old favorite from the American South.

Two parts Bourbon or rye whiskey

One part fresh lemon or lime juice

A teaspoon of sugar per glass

A cocktail cherry

A slice of orange

Ice cubes

◆ Place five or six ice cubes in a cocktail shaker, add the whiskey, lemon or lime juice and sugar.
◆ Shake well and strain into a cocktail glass.
◆ Serve decorated with the slice of orange and a cocktail cherry speared together on a stick.

GALLIANO SOUR

One part Scotch whisky

One part Galliano

One part orange juice

Superfine sugar

Half a part lemon or lime juice

A slice of orange

Ice cubes

◆ Place eight ice cubes in a cocktail shaker and add all the liquid ingredients.
◆ Shake well.
◆ Frost the rim of a cocktail glass with the sugar, strain the cocktail carefully into the glass, taking care not to disturb the frosting.
◆ Decorate with the orange slice.

MANHATTAN

Three parts whiskey

One part sweet vermouth

A cocktail cherry

Ice cubes

◆ Place six ice cubes in a bar glass and add the whiskey and vermouth.
◆ Stir thoroughly, then strain into a chilled lowball glass.
◆ Decorate with a cocktail cherry on a stick.

Galliano Sour, Manhattan and Whiskey Sour

NEW YORKER

Three parts whiskey

One part lime juice (fresh if possible)

Half a teaspoon of superfine sugar per glass

A dash of grenadine per glass

A twist of orange

Crushed ice

◆ Place a cup of crushed ice in a cocktail shaker and add the whiskey, lime juice, sugar and dash of grenadine.
◆ Shake well and strain into a chilled cocktail glass.
◆ Decorate with a twist of orange.

BENEDICT

Three parts Scotch whisky

One part Bénédictine

Ginger ale

A slice of lemon

Ice cubes

◆ Place two ice cubes in a bar glass, add the whisky and Bénédictine, stir well and strain into a lowball glass.
◆ Top off with ginger ale and decorate with a slice of lemon.

Benedict and New Yorker

MINT JULEP

It takes quite a bit of time to prepare a good julep, so good hosts often make several before the guests arrive, and keep them in the freezer.

A tankard of Bourbon (!)

A large bunch of fresh mint

A teaspoon of sugar

Two tablespoons of water

A teaspoon of Barbados rum

Crushed ice

◆ Tear up about 15 mint leaves to release the flavor, and drop them into a beer tankard or glass.
◆ Add the sugar and water and stir until the mint is thoroughly crushed and the sugar is dissolved. Discard the mint.
◆ Now fill the tankard with finely crushed ice and pour in enough Bourbon to reach to about an inch from the rim of the tankard.
◆ Stir the mixture well, then float a teaspoon of rum on the surface.
◆ Decorate with sprigs of mint leaves, arranged so the drinker's nose sinks into them when he (or she) takes a sip of the julep.

Mint Julep

BRAINSTORM

One part Scotch whisky

One part Bénédictine

One part dry vermouth

A slice of orange

Crushed ice

◆ Place three tablespoons of crushed ice in a bar glass.
◆ Pour the whisky, Bénédictine and vermouth over the ice.
◆ Stir and strain into a cocktail glass, then serve decorated with the orange slice.

Brainstorm, Three Rivers and Oh, Henry!

OH, HENRY!

Three parts whiskey

Half a part Bénédictine

Six parts ginger ale

A slice of lemon

Ice cubes

◆ Fill a highball glass with cubes of ice and add the whiskey, Bénédictine and ginger ale.
◆ Stir gently, but enough to ensure proper mixing without losing the bubbles.
◆ Decorate with a slice of lemon.

RUSTY NAIL

This drink probably gets its name from its rusty color.

Two parts Scotch whisky

One part Drambuie

A twist of lemon

Ice cubes

◆ Fill a cocktail glass with ice cubes.
◆ Add the whisky and Drambuie and stir well. Serve decorated with a twist of lemon.

NEW ORLEANS

Three parts Bourbon

One part Pernod

Three dashes of Angostura bitters per glass

A dash of orange bitters per glass

A dash of Anisette per glass

A teaspoon of sugar syrup (or less, to taste) per glass

A twist of lemon

Crushed ice

◆ Place a cup of crushed ice in a cocktail shaker. Add the Bourbon, Pernod, Angostura and orange bitters, Anisette and sugar syrup.
◆ Shake well.
◆ Fill a lowball glass with ice cubes and strain the cocktail over them.
◆ Decorate with a twist of lemon.

WALDORF COCKTAIL

There's no doubt about the hotel in which this cocktail originated.

Two parts Bourbon whiskey

One part Pernod

One part sweet vermouth

A dash of Angostura bitters per glass

Crushed ice

◆ Place a cup of crushed ice in a bar glass and add the whiskey, Pernod, vermouth and bitters.
◆ Stir well and strain into a chilled cocktail glass.
◆ Serve undecorated.

Rusty Nail, Waldorf Cocktail and New Orleans

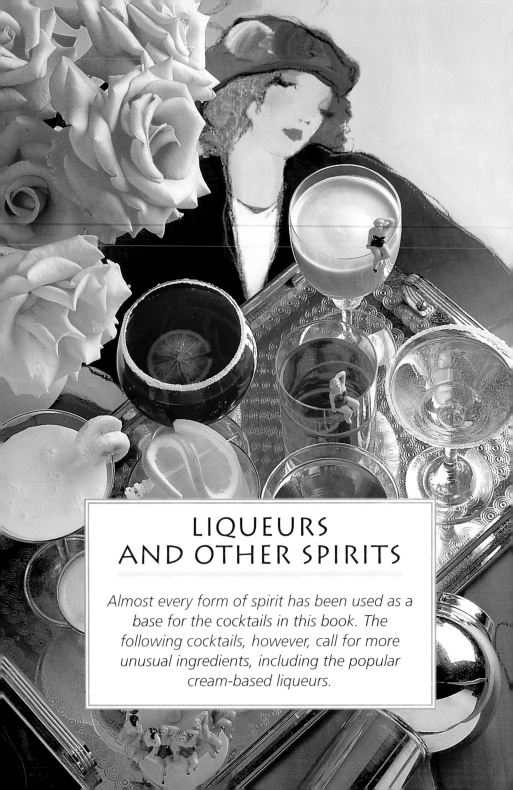

LIQUEURS
AND OTHER SPIRITS

Almost every form of spirit has been used as a base for the cocktails in this book. The following cocktails, however, call for more unusual ingredients, including the popular cream-based liqueurs.

BANANA MINT COCKTAIL

The combination of banana and mint makes an irresistible cocktail and a perfect substitute for dessert.

One part Crème de Banane

One part white Crème de Menthe

One part cream

Two slices of banana (optional)

Crushed ice

◆ Place four ice cubes in a cocktail shaker, add the Crème de Banane, Crème de Menthe and cream and shake well.
◆ Place a scoop of crushed ice in a cocktail glass and strain the cocktail over it.
◆ Serve undecorated, or with two slices of banana.

Banana Mint Cocktail

SANGRIA

In its most basic form, Sangria is fruit juice added to red wine. It can be made in large quantities and served as a punch, usually with soda water to add fizz, and sometimes with brandy for extra kick. Or it can be served as an individual cocktail, as described here.

Four parts red wine

One part sugar syrup

Two parts orange juice

One thin slice of lime

Sugar

Ice cubes

◆ Place four ice cubes in a mixing glass and add the wine, sugar syrup and orange juice. Stir well.
◆ Frost the rim of a large wine glass with sugar and strain the mixture carefully into the glass.
◆ Decorate with the slice of lime and serve.

BANSHEE

One part Crème de Cacao

One part Crème de Banane

One part cream

A dash of gomme syrup per glass

A slice of kiwi fruit (optional)

Crushed ice

◆ Place all the liquid ingredients into a blender, including a scoop of crushed ice, and blend for about five seconds. Alternatively, blend by shaking very well in a cocktail shaker for at least 10 seconds.
◆ Pour into a cocktail glass.
◆ Serve undecorated, or add a slice of kiwi fruit.

Sangria and Banshee

BLACK SHEEP

Here's another dark and mysterious-looking drink for very late at night.

One part Kahlúa

Two parts stout

Two parts Glayva

Thick cream

Ice cubes

◆ Place four ice cubes in a bar glass, add the Kahlúa, stout and Glayva (a Scotch whisky liqueur; you can substitute Drambuie if you wish) and stir well.
◆ Strain into an old-fashioned glass and float the thick cream on the top.

Black Sheep

BLOODY BULL

This may sound dreadful, but if you enjoy a Bloody Mary, you might find this combination even more exciting.

One part tequila

Two parts tomato juice

Two parts cold beef stock

A squeeze of lemon juice per glass

Celery leaves

A slice of lemon

Ice cubes

◆ Place four ice cubes in a cocktail mixing glass, add the tequila, tomato juice, beef stock and a squeeze of lemon juice.
◆ Stir thoroughly, then strain into a lowball glass.
◆ Decorate with celery leaves and a slice of lemon.

Bloody Bull

DANISH MARY

This is really just a Danish version of the old Bloody Mary, with the fiery aquavit instead of vodka.

One part aquavit

One small can tomato juice

Two dashes of Worcestershire sauce per glass

Celery salt

Lemon juice

A thin stick of celery

Ice cubes

◆ Place five ice cubes in a cocktail shaker, add the aquavit, tomato juice, two dashes of Worcestershire sauce, celery salt to taste and a squeeze or two of lemon juice.
◆ Shake well, then strain into a highball glass.
◆ Decorate with the stick of celery.

CHARLESTON

One part Mandarine Napoléon

One part cherry brandy

Lemonade

Ice cubes

◆ Place the Mandarine Napoléon and cherry brandy in a bar glass and stir.
◆ Fill a highball glass with ice cubes and pour the cocktail over them.
◆ Top off with lemonade and serve undecorated.

BLUE HAWAIIAN

Blue drinks are always fascinating as there is very little that we normally drink – or eat – that is blue.

One part Blue Curaçao

Two parts Coconut Cream

Two parts light rum

Four parts pineapple juice

A thin slice of pineapple (optional)

Crushed ice

◆ Place two large tablespoons of crushed ice in a blender, add the Curaçao, Coconut Cream, rum and pineapple juice and blend for about ten seconds.
◆ Serve in a large wine glass either undecorated or decorated with a thin slice of pineapple.

Blue Hawaiian, Charleston and Danish Mary

CALVADOS COCKTAIL

Calvados is a heady spirit made from distilled apple cider and is very popular in Brittany. This apple brandy forms the base for some very exciting cocktails.

Two parts Calvados

One part Cointreau

Two parts orange juice

One part orange bitters

A slice of orange

Ice cubes

◆ Place four or five cubes of ice in a cocktail shaker, add the Calvados, Cointreau, orange juice and orange bitters and shake well.
◆ Strain into a lowball glass and decorate with a slice of orange.

Calvados Cocktail

FUZZY NAVEL

There are several variations on this delicious theme, but the basic ingredients remain Peach Schnapps and fresh orange juice. Sometimes vodka is added to give it an extra kick. We offer the high-powered version.

One part vodka

One part Peach Schnapps

Six parts fresh orange juice

A slice of orange

Ice cubes

◆ Place five cubes of ice in a cocktail shaker and add the vodka, Peach Schnapps and orange juice.
◆ Shake well, then strain into a cocktail glass. Decorate with a slice of orange.

Fuzzy Navel

JOHNNIE

Three parts sloe gin

One part Curaçao

Two dashes of Anisette per glass

Ice cubes

◆ Place four ice cubes in a cocktail shaker, add the sloe gin, Curaçao and dashes of Anisette. Shake well, then strain into a cocktail glass.

MARGARITA

Three parts tequila

One part Triple Sec

One part lime juice

Salt

Crushed ice and ice cubes

◆ Place a scoop of crushed ice in a blender, add the tequila, Triple Sec and lime juice and blend for five seconds.
◆ Frost the rim of a cocktail glass with salt, add a couple of ice cubes and strain the cocktail over them carefully.

Calypso Cocktail, Margarita, Johnnie and Blue Negligee

BLUE NEGLIGEE

This one pleases the eyes almost as much as it pleases the palate.

One part green Chartreuse

One part Parfait Amour

One part ouzo

A cocktail cherry

Crushed ice

◆ Place two spoons of crushed ice in a bar glass, add the Chartreuse, Parfait Amour and ouzo.
◆ Stir well, then strain into a cocktail glass.
◆ Drop in a cocktail cherry and serve immediately.

CALYPSO COCKTAIL

One part Orange Curaçao

Ginger ale

A slice of lemon

Ice cubes

◆ Fill a highball glass with ice cubes, pour in the Orange Curaçao and top off with ginger ale.
◆ Decorate with a slice of lemon.

STEEPLEJACK

One part Calvados

*One and a half parts chilled
apple juice*

One and a half parts soda water

*A teaspoon of lime juice
per glass*

A slice of lime or lemon

Ice cubes

◆ Pour the Calvados, apple juice,
soda water and lime juice into a
bar glass.
◆ Stir, then pour the mixture into
a highball glass. It should half fill
the glass.
◆ Add enough ice to fill the glass
to the brim, and decorate with a
slice of lime or lemon.

Steeplejack

LA JOLLA

This is a fiery concoction based on that most fiery of Italian spirits, grappa. Drink it with caution!

Three parts grappa

One part Crème de Banane

One part lemon juice

A splash of orange juice per glass

A slice of orange

Ice cubes

◆ Place four ice cubes in a cocktail shaker, add the grappa, Crème de Banane, lemon juice and orange juice and shake well.
◆ Strain into a cocktail glass and decorate with a slice of orange.

La Jolla

COMFORTABLE SCREW

This is a naughty variation of the Screwdriver, using Southern Comfort instead of vodka.

One part Southern Comfort

Six parts orange juice

A banana (optional)

Ice cubes

♦ Place five ice cubes in a cocktail shaker. Add the Southern Comfort and orange juice.
♦ Shake well, then strain into a lowball glass.
♦ Decorate imaginatively with a banana and serve.

Comfortable Screw

EL DIABLO

Four parts tequila

One part lime juice

One part Curaçao

A teaspoon of Crème de Cassis per glass

Chilled soda water

A slice of lime or lemon

Ice cubes

◆ Place five or six ice cubes in a cocktail shaker and add the tequila, lime juice, Curaçao, and Crème de Cassis.
◆ Shake well, then strain into a highball glass half filled with ice .
◆ Fill the glass with chilled soda, stir gently and decorate with the slice of lime or lemon.

El Diablo

CHAMPAGNE COCKTAILS

*Champagne is the queen of wines and mixes
well with almost any fruit juice. This makes it
an ideal cocktail base. Remember, though, that
much of Queen Champagne's charm is in her
bubbles, so avoid shaking a Champagne-based
cocktail as this will dispel the sparkle.*

BLACK PRINCE

Champagne seems to blend well with almost any other fruit-based drink. Try this for a dramatic one.

One part blackberry liqueur

A dash of lemon or lime juice

Brut Champagne (or any very dry sparkling wine)

◆ Chill a Champagne flute and pour in the blackberry liqueur.
◆ Add the lemon or lime juice.
◆ Carefully top off with Champagne, keeping the dark liquor at the bottom, and serve.

BLACK VELVET

This drink should be quaffed while the bubbles are at their liveliest.

One part stout

One part chilled Champagne

◆ Half fill a Paris goblet or Irish coffee glass with stout.
◆ Top up with Champagne (or dry sparkling wine).

Black Prince and Black Velvet

DIAMOND FIZZ

Here's the perfect drink for a sweltering hot day.

One part gin

The juice of half a lemon per glass

A teaspoon of superfine sugar per glass

Chilled Brut Champagne

Ice cubes

◆ Place five ice cubes in a cocktail shaker, add the gin, lemon juice and sugar and shake well.
◆ Strain into a tall glass, add the Champagne and two cubes of ice.

ROYAL SCREW

Who could possibly resist a drink with such a topical name?

One part brandy

One part chilled fresh orange juice

Chilled Brut Champagne

◆ Pour the brandy into a Champagne flute.
◆ Add the orange juice and stir.
◆ Top off with Champagne.

KIR ROYALE

Seven parts chilled Brut Champagne

One part raspberry liqueur (Framboise) or Crème de Cassis

A twist of lemon

◆ Fill a Champagne flute three-quarters full with Champagne.
◆ Add the liqueur and serve decorated with a twist of lemon.

LONDON SPECIAL

This is really just a way to add a touch of fun to Champagne.

A twist of orange

A cube of sugar

Angostura bitters

Chilled Brut Champagne

◆ In a Champagne glass, place the twist of orange, the sugar cube and two dashes of bitters.
◆ Top off with chilled Champagne and stir very gently.

Diamond Fizz, London Special, Kir Royale and Royal Screw

DEATH IN THE AFTERNOON

Tradition has it that this was Ernest Hemingway's favorite drink when he lived in Paris.

One part Pernod

Chilled Brut Champagne

Ice cubes

◆ Place two ice cubes in a Champagne flute and pour the Pernod over them.
◆ Gently add the chilled Champagne, then stir gently so as not to lose the sparkle.

Death in the Afternoon

PRINCE OF WALES

Royalty, of course, is expected to be associated with Champagne, that queen of wines. Here's a royal cocktail with a regal kick.

One part brandy

One part Madeira wine (or white muscatel)

Three drops of Curaçao per glass

Two dashes of Angostura bitters per glass

Chilled Brut Champagne

A slice of orange

Ice cubes

◆ Place five ice cubes in a cocktail shaker and add the brandy, sweet wine, drops of Curaçao and dashes of bitters.
◆ Shake well, then strain into a chilled Champagne flute.
◆ Fill up with Champagne and decorate with a slice of orange.

Prince of Wales

SHOOTERS

Shooters were invented by ingenious Canadian bartenders looking for a new way to keep out the cold winter air. After several of these lethal little numbers, who cares how cold it is outside? Remember when pouring shooters to get the ingredients in the right order, with the heavier ones at the bottom.

LOVE BITE

Ideally you should make two of these at a time, so partners can quaff them together. We cannot be held responsible for anything that happens afterwards.

Cherry liqueur

Parfait Amour

Sweet cream

◆ Pour the cherry liqueur into the bottom of the shot glass and then add the Parfait Amour.
◆ Top off with a teaspoon or so of cream.

THE B52

One part Kahlúa

One part white Crème de Menthe

One part Grand Marnier

◆ Starting with the Kahlúa, pour the ingredients gently over the back of a spoon into a shot glass, taking care not to let them mix.

The B52 and Love Bite

CACTUS FLOWER

Better have some ice water handy to put out the fire!

Tequila

Tabasco sauce

◆ Almost fill a shot glass with tequila, then gently trickle a layer of Tabasco sauce on the top.

Galliano Hot Shot and Cactus Flower

GALLIANO HOT SHOT

This is a warming little shooter to enjoy after a good meal.

Galliano

Hot, strong coffee

Cream

◆ Half fill a shot glass with Galliano, carefully pour in hot coffee, keeping the two liquids separate as far as possible.
◆ Trickle a layer of cream on top.
◆ If the coffee is too hot, you may have to sip this one.

BANANA BOMBER

Shooters may have been invented in chilly Canada, but here's a sultry little number for those who want a taste of the tropics.

Banana liqueur

Brandy

◆ Half fill the shot glass with banana liqueur, then trickle the brandy over the back of a spoon.

Banana Bomber and Bleeding Heart

BLEEDING HEART

Unlike most shooters, this one doesn't come in separate layers of color, but the red and yellow "marbling" effect is still dramatic.

One part Advokaat

One part cherry brandy

◆ Half fill a shot glass with Advokaat and gently trickle the cherry brandy on top.
◆ The red liquor will form veins of color through the Advokaat, hence the name.

SLIPPERY NIPPLE

This popular drink was invented by a bored winemaker whiling away a winter evening at the local pub.

One part Black Sambuca

One part Baileys Original Irish Cream

◆ Pour the Sambuca into a shot glass, then very gently trickle the Irish Cream over the back of a spoon, carefully so that the two do not mix.
◆ Take a deep breath and toss it down the hatch.

ALTERED STATES

One part Kahlúa

One part Baileys Original Irish Cream

One part pear liqueur

◆ Starting with the Kahlúa, pour each of the ingredients gently over the back of a teaspoon into a shot glass, taking care not to allow them to mix.
◆ There should be three distinct layers of color.

Slippery Nipple

GREEN AND GOLD

Here's a South African drink named after the colors of the famous Springbok rugby jerseys.

Passion fruit syrup

Green Crème de Menthe

A teaspoon of ouzo per glass

◆ Pour a little passion fruit syrup into the bottom of the glass.
◆ Gently add the Crème de Menthe, without letting the gold and green mix.
◆ Slip a teaspoon of ouzo on the top and toss it back.

HOT SHOTS

One part vodka

One part Peppermint Schnapps

Tabasco sauce

◆ Gently pour first the vodka and then the Schnapps into a shot glass.
◆ Add a few drops of Tabasco sauce.
◆ Stand clear and fire when ready.

Hot Shots and Green and Gold

NON-ALCOHOLIC COCKTAILS

Not all cocktails have to be alcoholic. Non-alcoholic cocktails are exciting, attractive – and safe – and, in fact, it makes good sense to appoint one member of the party to remain sober to drive home safely afterwards.

ORANGE FIZZ

You can sometimes buy ready-made sour mix, but it's fun to make your own. Just mix equal quantities of lemon and lime juice and sugar to taste, stirring until the sugar is dissolved. Keep a bottle handy in the bar. Here's a good way to use some.

One part sour mix (see above)

Five parts fresh orange juice

Soda water

Ice cubes

◆ Fill a highball glass with ice cubes.
◆ Pour in the sour mix and add the orange juice. Stir well to blend them.
◆ Top off with soda water and serve undecorated.

Orange Fizz

JOHN LEE SPECIAL

The juice of half a fresh lime

Cola

A slice of lime or lemon

Ice cubes

◆ Fill a highball glass with ice.
◆ Pour in the lime juice and then top off with cola. Stir gently.
◆ Slip the cut slice of lime or lemon over the glass rim and serve.

PUSSYFOOT

One part lemon juice

Two parts orange juice

Half an egg yolk per glass

Dash of grenadine per glass

A sprig of mint

A cocktail cherry

Ice cubes

◆ Pour all the liquid ingredients over eight ice cubes in a cocktail shaker and shake vigorously.
◆ Strain into a tall glass and serve decorated with the mint and a cherry.

VIRGIN MARY

As the name hints, this is a Bloody Mary without the sinful vodka. It's still a pleasant drink if you've been nominated to drive.

One can of tomato juice

Two tablespoons of lemon juice per glass

A dash of Tabasco sauce per glass

A dash of Worcestershire sauce per glass

Celery salt to taste

Pepper

A stick of celery

Ice cubes

◆ Place five cubes of ice in a cocktail shaker and add the tomato juice and lemon juice.
◆ Add the seasonings, varying the quantities to taste, and shake well.
◆ Strain into a large wine glass or lowball glass and serve with a stick of celery.

Pussyfoot, John Lee Special and Virgin Mary

GENTLE SEA BREEZE

One part cranberry juice

One part grapefruit juice

Crushed ice and ice cubes

◆ Place a cup of crushed ice in a blender (or cocktail shaker if there is no blender handy).
◆ Add the juices and blend or shake until frothy.
◆ Pour into a highball glass and add a few ice cubes.

LASSIE

Four parts plain liquid yogurt

A tablespoon of heavy cream per glass

Two tablespoons of superfine sugar per glass

A cocktail cherry

Ice cubes

◆ Half fill a cocktail shaker with ice cubes and add the yogurt, cream and sugar. Shake very well.
◆ Strain into a cocktail glass and decorate with a cherry on a stick.

PASSION FRUIT SPRITZER

Here's a quick and easy drink that will find instant appeal.

The juice of half a lemon

A small can of passion fruit juice

Soda water

Ice cubes

◆ Place four ice cubes in a lowball glass and pour in the lemon juice.
◆ Add the passion fruit juice to fill about a quarter of the glass.
◆ Top off with soda water and serve undecorated.

BLACK COW

Traditionally this is made with dark root beer, but a cola drink will suffice if root beer is unavailable.

Root beer or cola

Two scoops of vanilla ice cream

◆ Place the ice cream in a highball glass. Add the root beer (or cola) and stir gently.
◆ Serve with a straw and a spoon.

Gentle Sea Breeze, Lassie, Black Cow and Passion Fruit Spritzer

JUNGLE COOLER

Here's an attractive blend of fruit juices. You can add others, depending on what's available.

Four parts pineapple juice

Two parts fresh orange juice

One part passion fruit squash

One part coconut milk

A slice of pineapple

Crushed ice

◆ Place a cup of crushed ice in a cocktail shaker.
◆ Add all the fruit juices, including the coconut milk, and shake very well.
◆ Strain into a tall glass and decorate with the pineapple.

Jungle Cooler

FRUIT CUP

Two parts orange juice

Two parts grapefruit juice

Two parts pineapple juice

Two parts apple juice

Slices of apple, lemon, kiwi fruit, strawberry and orange

Ice cubes

◆ Half fill a cocktail shaker with ice cubes, add the fruit juices and shake well.
◆ Strain into a highball glass and arrange the slices of fruit decoratively.
◆ Serve with a colorful straw.

Fruit Cup

INDEX

125

ACKNOWLEDGMENTS

The author, photographer and publishers extend grateful thanks to the following people and corporations for their kind assistance:

Above All, Bric a Brac, Burr and Muir, Framing Factory, Hans Niehaus, Camilla Pollard, Serendipity, Stellenbosch Farmer's Winery and Peter Visser Interiors.